LEARNING GOD'S STORY OF GRACE

LEARNING GOD'S STORY OF GRACE

A Living Story Book

Elizabeth Reynolds Turnage

© 2011 by Elizabeth Reynolds Turnage

All rights reserved. No part of this book may be reproduced, stored in a retrieval system, or transmitted in any form or by any means—electronic, mechanical, photocopy, recording, or otherwise—except for brief quotations for the purpose of review or comment, without the prior permission of the publisher, P&R Publishing Company, P.O. Box 817, Phillipsburg, New Jersey 08865-0817.

Unless otherwise indicated, all Scripture quotations are from the HOLY BIBLE, NEW INTERNATIONAL VERSION®. NIV®. Copyright © 1973, 1978, 1984 by International Bible Society. Used by permission of Zondervan Publishing House. All rights reserved.

Scripture quotations marked (MSG) are taken from *The Message*. Copyright © 1993, 1994, 1995, 1996, 2000, 2001, 2002. Used by permission of NavPress publishing group.

Scripture quotations marked (NLT) are taken from the Holy Bible, New Living Translation, copyright 1996, 2004. Used by permission of Tyndale House Publishers, Inc., Wheaton, Illinois 60189. All rights reserved.

Scripture quotations marked (ESV) are from *ESV Bible* ® (*The Holy Bible, English Standard Version* ®). Copyright © 2001 by Crossway Bibles, a publishing ministry of Good News Publishers. Used by permission. All rights reserved.

Printed in the United States of America

ISBN: 978-1-59638-243-5

Contents

Foreword

Long before *Living Story* was a Bible study series, website, weekend retreat, coaching vehicle, and consulting practice, it was a way of life for my friend Elizabeth Turnage. Over the past several years, I've had the privilege of watching Elizabeth marinate in the gospel of God's grace and come alive to its radical and transforming implications. I'm thankful to see this firsthand, because the people I trust the most to tell me about Jesus are those who continually demonstrate just how much they need Jesus. Hypothetical grace only avails hypothetical sinners. Theoretical mercy only avails the theoretically broken. Metaphorical living water only quenches those who metaphorically thirst.

Quite literally, I saw *Living Story* become a seed, long before it even got planted. And since germination, this ministry has been growing as an expression of Elizabeth's growth in grace and understanding of the big narrative that runs from Genesis through Revelation. That journey and process will be evident to you in the following pages and exercises.

Here's the main thing that excites me about the gift Elizabeth offers us. She shows us the vital connection between the main story line of the Bible and our stories of God's transforming grace. In short, Elizabeth helps us find our place in God's story–God's *Living Story* of redemption and restoration. Each of us is called to be a character in and a carrier of this amazing story. Indeed, the gospel runs to us and through us, to the glory of God.

Sometimes God's grace and personal "story work" are presented in a vacuum, without any reference or clear connection to God's transforming kingdom. The impression is given that the gospel is primarily a means for helping us escape the prison house of legalism, bad self-imaging, and the talons of our broken family systems. The net result is liberated Christians who throw off the shackles of shame and guilt, reject performance-based living, and finally learn to be their own person. Not that all of that is bad, but the gospel calls us to far richer categories, and a much bigger vision and story.

On the other hand, the gospel is also presented, at times, almost exclusively in terms of fulfilling the Great Commission and engaging in issues of moral reform and social justice, while bypassing the dark continent of our own hearts. This results in dutiful Christians with little depth and authenticity, busy churches full of pragmatic agendas and type A personalities, and in time, empty believers marked more by posing and pretending than by faith expressing itself in love. This simply will not do.

Living Story celebrates God's commitment to make all things new through the person and work of Jesus–individuals, marriages, families, neighborhoods, and cities. Elizabeth helps us hear the echoes of Eden–the world for which God originally made us. She also helps us grieve the evidences of sin and death, rejoice in the provision of God's Son and God's gospel, and hope for the sure arrival of the new heaven and new earth. I am very thankful for my friend's hard work and tenderness of heart–as a person and as a servant of Jesus on the behalf of many, as she clearly is.

Scotty Smith

Acknowledgments

One of my favorite story questions is, "How did I get *here*—to this place in my story?" The answer always involves characters who impacted the plot. I would like to thank everyone who played a part in the creation of this book, and in particular the following:

Mary Jacqueline McIntyre Reynolds: Mom. You birthed persistence and modeled determination in the face of adversity.

Robert Charles Reynolds Sr.: Dad. You introduced me to a love for the written word.

Kirby Turnage III: My dear story partner. You have walked this wild and wondrous story of redemption with me for over half my life. Thank you, my beloved, for believing in the power of the gospel in me more than I did.

Kirby, Jackie, Mary Elizabeth, and Robert Turnage: Children of my heart. You have lived redemption before my eyes. You have loved me, humored me, humbled me, and called me to be the mother I could only be through the work of Christ!

Hope Parker, Lalla Pierce, Cheryl Simcox, and Christie Tilley: My story sisters. For over a decade, you have brought the gospel to me, labored with me, prayed for me, loved me so very faithfully, and shared "really good stories" with me.

Scotty and Darlene Smith: Pastor and friend. You have shown me that teaching the story of grace means nothing if you don't live it.

Dan and Becky Allender: Teacher and friend. You have shown me the gospel hope of telling true stories. You have wept and rejoiced with me over the brokenness and beauty of this fallen and far more redeemed world.

Bill Puryear III: Faithful brother and tough coach. You kindly blocked all my favorite escape routes so this book could begin and be completed.

Marvin Padgett and P&R Publishing: Editor and publisher. You had a vision for this work's gospel-spreading potential, and you labored gloriously with me to make it happen.

INTRODUCTION

LEARNING STORY

Who am I? Where did I come from? Is there any meaning and purpose to my life? Whether you're seventy or seventeen, punk or prep, Native American or native African, these are the questions that rumble in our souls, according to anthropologists. The Bible acknowledges these questions too and exhorts us to know and tell our story. Remembering and communicating our history reminds us of the essential realities that influence how we live our daily lives.

My friend Joni grew up hearing her father shout, "I hate you! I wish you had never been born!" She needs to know that while she is a sinner, she was created with dignity and re-created through redemption. These parts of her story allow her to walk upright, proud, and free of fear because the God who created her delights in her even if her earthly father doesn't. Another friend tends to be judgmental because he focuses on the sins of others and minimizes his own. He needs to remember the story of Scripture, which explains our sin as the demand to have our way. When he sees his sinful heart though the lens of God's redemptive love, he doesn't spend so much time scrutinizing the sins and failures of others.

Both friends need to know the grand narrative Scripture tells. The gospel story sings a song of redemption with the following four parts:

1. Creation tells us who we are, male and female, created in the image of God. It is characterized by shalom—peace, wholeness, harmony. Everything is the way it's supposed to be.
2. The fall tells us why we struggle with sin and live in frustration. It is characterized by wrecked shalom—sin has divided what was meant to be together, distorted beauty, and deconstructed wholeness. The effects of the fall are compounded when we try to restore shalom by turning to people, places, or things that make us feel significant. The Bible calls this idolatry.
3. Redemption tells of the sinless Savior, Jesus Christ, who rescued us from sin and death by living as a human, dying, and rising from the dead. This wild story of God's grace means that anyone who trusts in Christ for salvation is transformed to live the free life we were created to live. In this part of the story, shalom is partially restored: re-location, re-conciliation, and re-creation characterize our lives, even though the final day of restoration is still to come.
4. Consummation, the grand finale of the story, brings full restoration and begins our truest story: the life of harmony and wholeness in worship of the triune God.

Scripture shows us that our stories matter. Our life narratives follow the rhythm of God's story of grace: a period of shalom, the wrecking or unraveling of shalom, further deconstruction as we attempt to restore shalom on our own terms, and finally rescue and partial restoration of shalom with full restoration to come.

History is . . . a story written by the finger of God.

—C.S. Lewis, "Historicism"

Living Story

Scripture calls us to learn and rehearse God's story of grace, because doing so calls us to live a life of faith, hope, and love—the essence of worship:

- Faith means trusting in God for life and hope rather than other gods.
- Hope means believing God is doing brand new things in the midst of wrecked shalom.
- Love is living and telling our story to a broken world sorely in need of a life-transforming story.

We need to learn God's story of grace in order to live it. Learning doesn't mean simply studying hard or pounding information into our minds. Learning means knowing. When the Bible speaks of knowing, it refers to a deep connection involving heart and mind. To know God is to be intimately connected with him. As we consider both the big story God has written in Scripture and the particular stories he is writing in our lives, we come to know God more deeply and love him more fully.

The Guide

This Bible study aims to bring the transforming power of the gospel to bear on your life. As you interact with this

---

Maybe nothing is more important than that we keep track, you and I, of these stories of who we are and where we have come from and the people we have met along the way because it is precisely through these stories in all their particularity . . . that God makes himself known to each of us most powerfully and personally.

—Frederick Buechner, *Telling Secrets: A Memoir*

material, I hope you will experience the freedom to live in God's story of grace with deeper faith, greater hope, and more passionate love. The format is designed to take you into the grand narrative of Scripture, your story, and others' stories by giving you opportunities to pray and live what you are studying. The following sections are found in each chapter to help you go deeper:

Engaging Scripture. Here you will focus on a passage or story from Scripture and answer questions for insight, reflection, and discussion. This draws us to worship God and follow Christ.

Theological Theme. This section discusses a theme that God consistently reveals through Scripture.

Entering Your Story. This section takes the passage and shifts the focus to what God is writing in your story. Here you will be given opportunities to write and tell your story.

Living Story. This section invites you to reflect on how you will live out the gospel in the topic being explored.

Praying Story. The final section offers an opportunity to write or say prayers regarding the story.

In addition to the format, here are a few suggestions to help you get the most out of this book.

Just do it! As a former stoic, I used to embrace this Nike slogan, but it didn't always lead to love. While I don't want you to fall into the trap of doing duty, I want you to engage the material. If the only thing you can do is read the Scripture, make sure you do that. The Bible is the living Word of God. Unlike any self-help book, just reading it transforms you! But please, do more.

Interact with the questions. The studies are divided into suggested amounts of material to cover over a five-day period. This gives you two extra days! Use the space in the book, or if you need more room, get a journal or create a document on your computer for walking through this guide. Let the questions wander around in your brain as you commute to work or clean the kitchen, and then write some things down. You may think you don't need to write anything down, but trust me–or at least trust cognition theorists–we learn, understand, and grow as we write.

Pray. Ask the Holy Spirit, whom God has given as "the helper" to come alongside you, to be your primary guide in the process of learning and living his story. Specific exercises for prayer are provided in each chapter.

Tell and listen. Each individual reflects God's story of grace in a unique way. Gift others by sharing your responses and your story. If you tend to be more talkative, make room for the quieter ones to speak. Always listen carefully to others.

Enjoy. We were made to worship, to give and receive delight in God's story of grace. My deepest hope is that you will enjoy being transformed by the gospel, the amazing true story in which we are called to live and love.

1

Story Matters

KEY THEMES:

- Remembering and rehearsing God's story of grace helps us turn away from our sin to trust in God (repentance).
- Remembering God's amazing grace draws us to live a life of obedience out of our gratitude for his rescue in our lives.

DAY 1

It was early, and I kept the lights low in the kitchen as I began my daily ritual. While the coffee brewed, I grabbed the small sample bottle of anti-inflammatory medication I took to ease body aches. Without looking, I reached in to remove a pill. The cotton felt unusually thick and sticky. I shook the bottle. No rattle. That's when I turned on the light and tried to rouse my sleep-laden eyes to look. What I found did not surprise me as much as it might surprise you. Stuck in the pill bottle instead of cotton was a large, white marshmallow!

As odd as it was, I guessed pretty quickly what had happened. One of my four children must have found the empty bottle and decided to replace the "marshmallow" that I regularly pulled out of it.

God's story matters. Your story matters too. But our stories don't always make much sense to us. Sometimes we can easily figure out an explanation while other times we continue to shake our heads (or our fists) for days at our confusion or disappointment. Psalm 78 shows us how much our story matters by revealing two major characteristics of the biblical narrative.

- First, the Bible as a whole is a very puzzling but absolutely true tale.
- Second, even the simplest stories reveal profound truths.

With these ideas in mind, let's look at Psalm 78 to understand how much our story matters.

Engaging Scripture: Psalm 78

Background

Genre. A Psalm: from the Hebrew word *tehillim*, which means "praise." Ironically, over 70 percent of Psalms are actually laments. God wants to hear our full expression of praise, doubt, fear, and hope. He takes all of our emotions and brings them to praise.

Our greatest desire, greater even than the desire for happiness, is that our lives mean something. This desire for meaning is the originating impulse of story. We tell stories because we hope to find or create significant connections between things. Stories link past, present, and future in a way that tells us where we have been (even before we were born), where we are, and where we could be going.

—Daniel Taylor, *The Healing Power of Stories*

Context. Psalms are Hebrew poems that are meant to be sung in community worship. These weren't just private prayers to God. Hebrew poetry uses a lot of repetition and rhythm, so we may not always get the full effect in English.

Psalm 78: A Story to Remember

Psalm 78 is a long Psalm calling the Israelites to remember the story of God's grace and mercy. It depicts Israel's history as one of forgetfulness and disobedience followed by remembrance and repentance. Set aside ten minutes to read the whole Psalm to get a sense of the redundancy of Israel's cycles of sin and the relentlessness of God's mercy and forgiveness. This pattern offers good news to us today, particularly because Christ the Savior brought an end to the cycle of disobedience and rebellion.

1. Read Psalm 78. Choose a verse you would like to memorize for this particular study. Find one that feels personal to you and your story. Write it here or on a note card or sticky note.

The following is an outline of Psalm 78 to help you see some of the cycles:

Part 1: A Call to Remember and Tell (vv. 1-8)
Part 2: Forgetting His Works and Wonders (vv. 9-16)
Part 3: Sin and Disbelief (vv. 17-31)
Part 4: Repentance, False Repentance, and God's Mercy (vv. 32-39)
Part 5: More Forgetting and Remembering (vv. 40-64)
Part 6: End of Story: God's Mercy (vv. 65-72)

2. Part 1: Read verses 1-8.

   a. Asaph asks the people to listen to his teaching. What is the content of this teaching (vv. 2-4)? What do the words "hidden lessons" and "parables" suggest to you about the Israelites' history?

The psalms express every emotion that human beings experience. The laments articulate our fear, despair, shame, and anger. The hymns express joy, love, and confidence. As we read the words of the psalmist, they become our own. They help us understand what is going on inside of us. But even more, they minister to us as they direct us toward God.

—Tremper Longman III, *How to Read the Psalms*

b. Describe some of the effects rehearsing this history will have (vv. 6–8). How has telling or hearing stories of rescue and redemption impacted you?

3. Part 2: Read verses 9–16.

   a. Name some of the marvels/miracles the Ephraimites forgot (vv. 13-16). What did forgetting lead them to do (vv. 9–11)?

b. Do you ever forget stories of how you have been rescued? What happens when you forget?

DAY 2

1. Part 3: Read verses 17–31.

   a. How do the Israelites' sin and disbelief grow and worsen (vv. 17–20)?

   b. How does God respond? Name some elements of provision and some elements of discipline (vv. 21–32).

Theological Theme: Repentance

The word *repent* has gotten a bad rap from street preachers who stand on the corner screaming it. But when understood in the context of the grand narrative of Scripture, it becomes an invitation to freedom. Repentance means to turn away from doing things our own way in order to follow God and rest in his provision and plan for our lives. Psalm 78 invites us to think about this true repentance that is found throughout the Bible.

Parts four and five of the psalm tell of God's chosen people raising their fists at him, shouting their unbelief, and turning their backs on his kind provision. God waits patiently for them to turn back toward him, and when they do not, he brings discipline with the purpose of leading them to repentance.

The people initially seem to repent, but verse 36 tells us their repentance only appeared to be sincere. In fact, they were flattering God, or as Eugene Peterson puts it in *The Message*, "They didn't mean a word of it; they lied through their teeth the whole time. They could not have cared less about him, wanted nothing to do with his Covenant." False repentance often involves people working harder to do better in their own effort. It is often motivated by a desire to stay out of trouble and is marked by a goal of keeping the peace.

True repentance comes from the heart. It trusts in our Savior, Jesus Christ, to bring about the change, while it cooperates with God in that transformation. Its motivation is godly sorrow, a real sense of having harmed God by living life our own way. The end goal is to restore shalom, which means hoping and looking for reconciliation between God and others.

c. Why did God respond the way he did? What kind of response was he hoping to evoke? (Read Heb. 12: 5–11.)

2. Parts 4 and 5: Read verses 32–64.

a. What result does God's punishment have (vv. 32–37)?

b. What reason does the psalmist give for God's choice not to destroy the Israelites? What does this show us about ourselves? What does it show us about God and the basis for our salvation (vv. 38–39)?

3. Part 6: Read verses 65–72.

   a. The psalm ends depicting God's amazing grace to the Israelites. What does God do for the Israelites (vv. 68–70)?

   b. What is hopeful about the way the psalm ends (vv. 70–72)?

Asaph tells us a very strange story in Psalm 78. In verse 2, the Hebrew words for "story" are *mashal* and *chiydah*, which suggest puzzles, hard questions, and riddles. Asaph may have chosen these words to communicate that Israel has a puzzling history. Perhaps he is saying, "Listen to this history and try to explain why people would repeatedly reject a God who not only performs such signs, wonders, and miracles, but who bothers to retrieve this stubborn, disobedient people. What kind of sense does it make to be so faithless and fickle in light of the Lord's unfailing love and kindness? And what kind of sense does it make to be so faithful and loving in light of the Israelites' faithlessness and forgetfulness?"

❁ Review your memory verse. Say it aloud three times.

DAY 3 & DAY 4

Entering Your Story

A "Living Stone" Story

Joshua 4 tells a story in which the Israelites are instructed to gather stones from the riverbed God had dried up so they could cross it. It seems a little bizarre, but Joshua explains the following to his people: "In the future, when your children ask you, 'What do these stones mean?' tell them that the flow of the Jordan was cut off before the ark of the covenant of the Lord. When it crossed the Jordan, the waters of the Jordan were cut off. These stones are to be a memorial to the people of Israel forever" (Josh. 4:6-7). Our stories are our memorials of what God has done for us. As we learn to collect and recollect them, our faith will grow. The following story is an example:

> Many years ago a tragedy struck our church family. Our youth pastor's wife had been badly burned in a grease fire. With burns covering 38 percent of her body, she lay like a bandaged mummy in the burn treatment center nearby; her hope for full recovery looked bleak. I was struggling with God over the situation, praying my childish criticisms. "If you are going to treat these two dear young servants like this, I quit! Why should I trust you when you let things like this happen? What kind of God are you?"
>
> I was depressed and angry, but as a mother, I could not stay in my study sobbing all afternoon. I had to take my children to swim lessons at the local health club. I sat glumly at the edge of the pool, feet dangling in the water, staring into it hoping for clarity to come. A gentleman came and stood next to me, watching his grandson. He remarked, "Boy, I had a tough run tonight!" I looked toward him and found myself eye level with his right leg, which bore a ghastly scar beginning near his ankle and stretching up above his knee. The scarred leg stood in a running shoe elevated by a platform. I knew this man, and I knew his story well. Because I knew his story, I had the strange urge

to laugh at his complaint of a tough run. God had placed beside me a living stone.

Let me explain my seemingly cruel urge to laugh. This man was one of my husband's former patients. About five years before, early on a Sunday morning, my husband, an orthopedic surgeon, was called into a horrible trauma involving this man. A local pastor, he had arisen well before dawn to complete a training run for the New York marathon before he led multiple church services. He was running on a major highway and a drunk driver had crossed the road and struck him from behind. After seeing the pastor's wound, Kip feared the injury might end in amputation of the limb–the leg was shattered, and the wound was full of road rash that could easily lead to infection. The idea that this man might ever run again did not cross Kip's mind.

And there he stood next to me, wondering like any other runner why his run had been difficult that evening. God had so healed him that he hardly gave a thought to the devastation that this leg had endured some five years before. It was a living stone–in living color and flesh–a picture to me of what God can do when all seems hopeless.

Choose one of the topics below to reflect on how your story matters. Question 1 takes you through any story. Question 2 is focused on a "Living Stone" story.

1. Think of some stories in your life that seem confusing.
   a. Without trying to explain them, write down what is confusing about them.

b. Write out one of the confusing stories of your life. Don't try to bring resolution, but consider writing a prayer at the end about what confuses you.

2. Write out a "Living Stone" story (see example above). Use the following guiding questions to get you started. Ask the Holy Spirit to help you remember and to write the story as you recall it.

   a. Can you think of a time when you felt doubt and desperation, but you were encouraged to set your hope anew on God?

   b. What was the difficult situation you faced?

c. Did God remind you of how he had rescued you in previous situations? If so, what was the reminder (some possibilities: a story, a visual reminder, a song)?

DAY 5

Living Story

1. Review Psalm 78:32–37. About the repentance of the Israelites, Eugene Peterson says, "They didn't mean a word of it; they lied through their teeth the whole time. They could not have cared less about him, wanted nothing to do with his Covenant" (MSG).

Repentance is not a decision of the will to do right instead of wrong. It's an internal shift in our perceived source of life. Ultimately repentance is a humble broken return to God, but there's a catch. We are utterly unable to do it. Repentance is not something we can decide to do and then do it; it's something God works in us. Then what's our part? Our part is getting ready for God to work repentance in us. Before God can turn us, we have to become deeply dissatisfied with the way things are now. That's where we're hungry for change and hopeful that change is possible.

—Dan Allender, *The Wounded Heart: Hope for Adult Victims of Childhood Sexual Abuse*

2. Consider the following pitfalls of false repentance, then check the traps you have fallen into. Make notes about when you recall doing any of the following:

- ☐ Feeling sorry about the consequences of your sin, but not the heart attitude underneath (being sorry you got caught, not sorry you did it).

- ☐ Focusing on doing better and working harder.

- ☐ Ignoring the heart attitude underlying the behavior–pride, self-righteousness, fear, or demandingness.

- ☐ Asking someone to forgive you so you can feel better about yourself.

3. Below is a list of marks of true repentance. Pray about these, remembering times of turning that were characterized by these attitudes. Ask God to continue to grow you in a lifestyle of repentance.

- ☐ Overwhelmed by God's grace.
- ☐ Humbled by the depths of demandingness in our own hearts.
- ☐ Feeling sorrow that we have hurt another in our sin.
- ☐ Knowing that only God can transform our hearts.
- ☐ Turning away from the things that make our hearts feel safe, secure, and significant and instead trusting in God to provide those things.

Praying Story

Choose one of the following options for praying the story of this chapter:

1. Write a prayer of thanksgiving, thanking God for some of the marvelous works he's done in your life.

The shortest road to repentance is remembrance. Let someone once recall what they used to be and reflect on what by God's grace they could be, and they will be led to repent, turning back from their sin to their Saviour.

—John Stott, *Authentic Christianity*

2. Write a prayer of repentance, telling God how you have tried to make life work apart from him. Ask him to help you experience his mercy and forgiveness just as it is depicted in his kindness, compassion, and forgiveness of the Israelites.

- Review your memory verse. Think of a creative way to share it with someone.

Moving Forward

Psalm 78 is one of many places in Scripture that calls us to remember and rehearse God's story of grace within our own stories. We are urged to learn and recite our stories:

1. To turn away from a stubborn persistence in living life on our own terms (repent)
2. To trust in God to rescue and redeem this wrecked world because he has done so in the past
3. To hope in God in the present because of what he has already done and what he will do on the final day
4. To love others well by showing grace because we have received mercy and by telling the story that is the basis for our faith and hope

As we have seen, God's grand narrative is indeed a strange and wonderful story. In the next chapter, we will consider its implications for our lives.

2

CREATION: THE BEGINNING OF SHALOM

KEY THEMES:

- The grand (and true) narrative of Scripture addresses core questions about life. Who is God? Who are we? Why is life so hard sometimes? How are we meant to live?
- Creation tells us that we were created with dignity in the image of God, for dominion over God's creation, and for delight in God and his creation.

DAY 1

"You are not allowed to hit your sister. It goes against everything you were made to be. God called you as a man to protect women, to honor them, and fight for them." So went a diatribe I oft repeated to my eldest son when he was between four and seven years old.

Many years later, when he was about thirteen, he asked me to talk with him. He had a story to tell me about intervening in a friend's self-destruction. Noticing how thin she was becoming, he asked her a few questions and learned that she was eating very little. He looked up eating disorders on the Internet, and realizing that her behavior was serious, he confronted her and insisted she tell her parents. She agreed, but asked if he would come with her to talk to them. As he finished the story, he said, "Well, I just wanted you to know because her parents might be calling you." After he told me, I sat stunned for a moment by a thirteen-year-old boy's courage and boldness in fighting lovingly for a woman's beauty.

How we live is directly related to how we were created. Though I could have just told my son that he couldn't beat up his sister "because I said so," I explained that, as a man, he simply wasn't created that way. When we understand how God created the world and us, we live boldly in the story of grace written into us.

ENGAGING SCRIPTURE: GENESIS 1-2

Background

Genre. Primeval history. This refers specifically to the history of the origin of the world, the nations, and the Israelites.

Title. "Genesis," a Greek word that means origin, source, race, or creation. In the Hebrew, the book is titled *bereshit,* which means

---

The Bible provides us with an overarching narrative in which all other narratives of the world are nested. The Bible is the story of God. The story of the world is first and foremost the story of God's activity in creating, sustaining, and redeeming the world to fulfill God's purposes for it.

—C.V. Gerkin, *Widening the Horizons*

"in the beginning." These names signify the purpose of Genesis–to tell the beginning of the grand narrative that defines God's chosen people.

1. Read Genesis 1 and 2. Choose a verse you would like to memorize for this particular study. Find one that feels personal to you and your story. Write it here or on a note card or a sticky note.

2. True or false? There are three creation stories in the Bible.

If you answered, "True," either you guessed it was a trick question or you already know that Genesis 1 and 2 tell two different, though complementary, creation stories. The third creation story is the story of new creation, the consummation of the grand narrative of Scripture, found in Revelation 21 and 22.

3. In Hebrew, the original language of the Old Testament, the first creation story is given to us in Genesis 1–2:4 in the form of a poem. Hebrew poetry often uses repetition to emphasize key points. Read Genesis 1–2:4 aloud and note any repetition you hear.

DAY 2

Genesis 2 offers another creation account. This second account is more like a story than a poem. It has a setting, characters, conflict, and resolution.

1. Briefly list the major elements of the Genesis 2 story:

   a. Setting (When and where?) (vv. 2:5–15):

   b. Characters (Who?) (vv. 2:5, 18–25):

   c. Conflict (What is the problem?) (vv. 2:18–20):

d. Resolution (How is the problem resolved? How does the story end?) (vv. 2:21–25):

Now let's look at the two creation accounts together to see what we learn about who God is, who we are, and what our purpose is.

2. Genesis 1 and 2 tell us much about the character of God. Read the verses listed below and write down what you learn about what God is like. Add any reflections on how that impacts you.

   a. God's existence: 1:1

   b. God's power: 1:3, 6, 9

c. God's plan: 1:26–31

d. God's nature: 1:26a, 27; 2:1–3

e. God's relationship to humankind: 1:27–28; 2:7, 15–17

f. God's sense of humor: 2:18–23

❁ Review your memory verse. Say it aloud three times.

DAY 3

What's our story? Genesis 1 and 2 reveal a lot about who we are, how we are meant to be, and what we are meant to do.

1. What do Genesis 1:26–27 and 2:24–25 tell us about the design of humans?

   a. 1:26–27

   b. 2:24-25

2. Name several purposes God has given humans (vv. 1:28–31).

The heavens declare the glory of God; the skies proclaim the work of his hands. Day after day they pour forth speech; night after night they display knowledge. There is no speech or language where their voice is not heard. Their voice goes out into all the earth, their words to the ends of the world.

—Psalm 19:1–4

Theological Theme: Creation

Creation tells us who God is, what the created cosmos is like, who we are, and what we are called to do.

God. Genesis 1 and 2 tell of a God who is distinct from, above, and outside of creation. God is Creator, Architect, King, and Owner of the cosmos. Though God is above and beyond his creation, he is also personal and relational and clearly delights in harmony, beauty, relationship, and rest.

The cosmos. Creation is harmonious, orderly, imaginative, and complete. All of creation (from the dormouse to the mountain moose, the dry desert to the flowing streams) reflects God's image, and in so doing, gives glory to God! Creation was made to worship—to bow down before the author and Creator of its story.

Humans. Humans are the crown of creation, not a last minute addition. We are the pinnacle of God's creation. Genesis shows God getting in the dust and forming mankind as a potter forms clay. It shows God in relationship creating mankind to reflect the image of the three-in-one God. We are made to be in relationship with one another and with God.

Our calling. Human beings are appointed as vice-regents in the King's created kingdom. We are blessed to bless and given the privilege to populate the cosmos with the creativity that reflects our Creators' mandate to be fruitful and multiply. The King has appointed us to rule over creation with our Creator's characteristic gentle strength. Just as the cosmos is created to reflect the glory of God, our greatest calling is to worship our Creator. We worship as sent ones, living our God-created mission in our assigned realms.

3. What do we learn about how men and women are made (vv. 2:18–23)?

Genesis 1 and 2 tell the story of "in the beginning," a time when God's creation enjoyed shalom. This Hebrew word signifies wholeness, harmony, integrity, and peace. He created humankind and declared us very good. We were created in *dignity* (in the image of God), with *difference* (male and female with complementary giftedness), and with *dominion* (a calling to steward the earth). We were made to worship God by enjoying intimate relationship, by multiplying creational beauty, and by spreading God's created shalom to the generations. All of these realities have great significance for our stories.

God is to be trusted as the sovereign Lord, with an eternal plan covering all events and destinies without exception, and with power to redeem, re-create and renew; such trust becomes rational when we remember that it is the almighty Creator that we are trusting. Realizing our moment-by-moment dependence on God the Creator for our very existence makes it appropriate to live lives of devotion, commitment, gratitude, and loyalty toward him, and scandalous not to. Godliness starts here, with God the sovereign Creator as the first focus of our thoughts.

—J.I. Packer, *Concise Theology*

DAY 4

Entering Your Story

A Shalom Story—"Fairlawn Express"

One way to think about what God is doing in our lives is to think of the structure of the Bible's grand narrative. Like the stories of the Bible, our stories begin in shalom, a season of harmony, peace, and fruitfulness.

> My parents had built their dream home in the small university town where my father had landed his first job as an English professor. New 70's style ranch homes sprouted in the red clay lots every day. My brother, his friends, and I spent many carefree childhood days playing in the vacant lots, covering ourselves with red clay. It was a time of innocence.
>
> One blissful summer Saturday, one of the neighborhood dads found an old wooden ladder and decided to make it into a great Saturday afternoon for the neighborhood kids. He attached lawn mower wheels along the ladder and hooked the whole thing up to the back of his riding lawn mower. He drove slowly through the neighborhood, beckoning the kids to come hitch a ride on the "Fairlawn Express." We all rode and whenever we saw another kid, we'd shout our invitation, "Fairlawn Express! Come ride the Fairlawn Express!"

Shalom is the human being dwelling at peace in all his or her relationships: with God, with self, with fellows, with nature . . . but the peace which is shalom is not merely the absence of hostility, not merely being in the right relationship. Shalom at its highest is enjoyment in one's relationships. A nation may be at peace with all its neighbors and yet be miserable in its poverty. To dwell in shalom is to enjoy living before God, to enjoy living in one's physical surroundings, to enjoy living with one's fellows, to enjoy life with oneself.

—Nicholas Wolterstorff, *Until Justice and Peace Embrace*

This is a memory of shalom, of a time when everything was right in my world. I had a sense that I was delightful, and I enjoyed a world of play and harmony. My parents were adding beauty to the earth by dreaming and building. In my experience of the world, relationships worked. In this season of my life, my world worked, and my story held together.

Think of a season or even a moment when you experienced the harmony and wholeness of shalom. Then use the following suggestions to guide reflection of your story:

1. Reread Nicholas Wolterstorff's description of shalom. List the types of enjoyment you experienced in that season or story (e.g., with friends, family, in health, surroundings, etc.).

2. Write a story of shalom in one to three paragraphs. What was the setting of the story (where and when did it take

place)? Who were the characters involved? What led to a feeling of harmony or wholeness?

- Review your memory verse.

DAY 5

Living Story

In this study, we learned that God created humankind with a design and a purpose: to be fruitful and multiply and to steward the earth.

What can you create? The following are examples: great presentations, money (you have the ability to make money or help other people make money), children, gourmet meals . . .

1. List anything and everything you like to create or have a gift to create. (Note: we don't always like some of the things we are gifted to do.)

2. Now choose two and think of a way you could bless others by sharing your creation.

3. We were created to steward, not exploit creation. Think of some possible projects you could do as a group to focus on stewarding creation.

Praying Story

Write a prayer expressing your thoughts about your creation. Try to include the following:

1. Praise God for his imagination and creativity in making *you* unique: "Thank you, Lord, for giving me a good sense of humor that blesses others."
2. Acknowledge ways that you doubt or disbelieve that you were made in his image: "Lord, because of my sin, it's sometimes hard to believe I was created with such glory, but I know it's true because it says it right here in Genesis 1 and 2."
3. Ask God to grow your vision of what it means to be created in the way you have been created. Ask the Spirit to reveal how your unique gifts can be used in the King's service.

Write your prayer here:

Moving Forward

We were made for shalom—created in glory to live in harmony and peace. We were made to worship God through loving him and multiplying beauty. We were made to enjoy God and his creation. Clearly that's not quite the way we live our lives today. In the next chapter, we will find out why.

3

The Fall: Wrecking Shalom

KEY THEMES:

- The fall reveals the impact of evil, in both our hearts and the world, and helps us understand why life is not the way it ought to be.
- Though the fall affected every aspect of good creation, it did not obliterate it. Because of God's grace, the restoration of creation is not only possible but certain.

DAY 1

Getting four children between the ages of one month to six years old dressed and ready for church required the Herculean efforts of both my husband and me. When he was on call and unavailable to help, I still managed to complete the feat, though I looked like I had run a marathon when I was done. It was not uncommon that in the moment we were walking out the door, one of the following things would happen: the baby would poop and his diaper would prove to be incompetent in its task; the baby would vomit all over my dress; the oldest two would start fighting; or the third child would have managed to lose one shoe on the way from her bedroom to the car.

I had a common response to these shalom-shattering events: I would throw up my hands in anger, look up to the heavens where I believed God must be reading the Sunday paper (I certainly didn't think he was counting the hairs on my head!), and I would scream, "I was made for more than this!" I was suffering the effects of the fall. In some ways, as we saw from the last chapter, my desperate cry was true. In other ways, my response was a sinful demand that life go according to *my* plan.

Genesis 3 tells the story of the fall: Adam and Eve listened to Satan, the evil one, and chose to ignore God's commands. They reached to take something they were convinced was even better than what God had already given them, fruit from the tree of knowledge of good and evil. They took life into their own hands, which resulted in shame, hiding, alienation from one another and God, blame, and the expulsion from the garden, among other things. Cornelius Plantinga, in his book *Not the Way It's Supposed to Be: A Breviary of Sin,* explains that shalom is the "way things ought to be." Evil and sin are the "vandalism of shalom."[1] Adam and Eve's sin affected the entire universe and everyone who lived thereafter, despoiling the beauty for which we were made. The fall tells the tragedy of our stories, but the good news is that God's grand narrative of grace does not end with this chapter.

Engaging Scripture: Genesis 3

Background

See chapter 2 for Genesis genre and background.

1. Cornelius Plantinga, *Not the Way It's Supposed to Be: A Breviary of Sin* (Grand Rapids: Eerdmans, 1995), 10-14.

The Fall. Sadly, the wholeness and harmony of all of creation came shattering to an end. Read Genesis 3, which tells part 2 of the grand narrative, the fall.

1. Read Genesis 3. Choose a verse you would like to memorize for this particular study. Find one that feels personal to you and your story. Write it here or on a note card or a sticky note.

2. Read Genesis 3:1–8. Outline the story according to the following structure:

    a. Characters (Who?):

Sin is fundamentally idolatrous. I do wrong things because my heart desires something more than the Lord. Sin produces a propensity toward idolatry in us all. . . . Sin is much more than doing the wrong thing. It begins with loving, worshiping, and serving the wrong thing.

—Paul David Tripp, *Instruments in the Redeemer's Hands*

b. Setting (When and where?):

c. Point of view (What are the different ways of seeing things and who presents them?):

d. Conflict (What is the problem?):

e. Resolution (How is the problem resolved? How does the story end?):

f. Theme (What are main ideas the story communicates?):

Evil is not inherent in the human condition: there once was a completely good creation and there will be again; hence, the restoration of creation is not impossible. Nothing in the world ought to be despaired of. Hope is grounded in the constant availability and the insistent presence of the good creation, even in those situations in which it is being terribly violated.

—Albert M. Wolters, *Creation Regained: Biblical Basics for a Reformational Worldview*

Let's look at the causes, consequences, and curses of the fall.

Causes

1. How does the serpent approach Eve? What does the Serpent (Satan) suggest to Eve about God's instruction (vv. 3:1, 4–5)? Mention some ways you have doubted the goodness of God's direction.

2. What error does Eve make in her response (v. 3:2)? What similar mistakes do we sometimes make regarding the Bible, Christianity, and God?

3. How does the tree look to Eve? What does this tell us about sin (v. 3:6)?

4. What do you think were the prime motivations for Eve to disobey God?

5. What part did Adam play in the story (vv. 3:1–6)?

DAY 2

Once Adam and Eve have sinned, the consequences quickly arrive: their eyes are opened, and they recognize and feel shame about their nakedness. They hear God walking in the garden and have to make a choice. They can turn themselves in, come clean with God, or they can try other ways to save themselves. Read Genesis 3:7-13.

Consequences

1. Name three ways Adam and Eve attempt to save themselves.

   (v. 7c):

   (v. 8b):

   (vv. 12-13):

2. What are some ways you have tried to escape the consequences of your sin? How well did they work for you?

Curses

1. How did the fall affect all of creation (vv.14–19)?

2. What curse did God deliver to the Serpent (Satan) (vv. 14–15)?

3. What painful result would Eve suffer because of the fall (v. 16)? If you are a woman, comment on how you have experienced this curse. If you are a man, comment on ways you have seen women experience it.

4. What painful result would Adam suffer because of the fall? If you are a man, comment on how you have experienced this curse. If you are a woman, comment on how you have seen men experience it.

Sin hurts other people and grieves God, but it also corrodes us. Sin is a form of self-abuse.

—Cornelius Plantinga, Jr., *Not the Way It's Supposed to Be: A Breviary of Sin*

Theological Theme: Sin

Sin, as Cornelius Plantinga states, is the "spoiling of shalom." Explaining the relationship between evil and sin, Plantinga says that whereas evil is "any spoiling of shalom," sin is a "subset of evil . . . evil for which someone is to blame."* Before the fall, Satan presented himself in the form of a serpent, and tempted Adam and Eve to commit sin, to choose rebellion against God's command. When they ate from the tree of the knowledge of good and evil, they didn't just commit sin, they also learned about evil. Their sin brought the impact of evil, the spoiling of shalom into the entire cosmos.

Genesis 3 and Romans 5 tell us that because of Adam and Eve's sin, we are born with a sin habit, a compulsion to sin. It corrupts, despoils, and wrecks the integrity of creation. It reproduces exponentially and divides, tearing apart what God has joined together.

J.I. Packer says sin is a "universal deformity: found at every point in every person (1 Kings 8:46; Rom. 3:9–23; 7:18; 1 John 1:8–10)." He says the moral deformity grows and changes; it is an "energy of irrational, negative, and rebellious reaction to God's call and command, a spirit of fighting God in order to play God. The root of sin is pride and enmity against God, the spirit seen in Adam's first transgression; and sinful acts always have behind them thoughts, motives, and desires that one way or another express the willful opposition of the fallen heart to God's claims on our lives."†

When we read these descriptions of sin, most of us will recognize the existence of this reality in our hearts and lives. Left to ourselves, we have no hope of escaping our commitment to write our stories our own way. Into the dark reality of our sinful hearts, God introduces a new plot twist, the true tale of a sinless man, God's own son, God incarnate, who died so that we could be freed from the bondage to sin.

* Cornelius Plantinga, *Not the Way It's Supposed to Be: A Breviary of Sin* (Grand Rapids: Eerdmans, 1995), 14.

† J. I. Packer, *Concise Theology: A Guide to Historic Christian Beliefs* (Wheaton, IL: Tyndale, 1993).

As ugly and painful as the fall narrative is, it is also a story of great beauty and hope. Even as dignity is lost and dominion is defiled, God is moving in mercy into the midst of the story. Answer the following questions to discover the many hopeful moments in Genesis 3:

5. "But the Lord God called to the man, 'Where are you?'" (v. 9). What is hopeful about this verse? What good news does it offer you regarding your sin?

6. Read what God says to the Serpent (Satan) in verse 15. What does this statement mean? What is hopeful about it?

7. How do you see God's mercy in the ending of the story (vv. 21-24)?

- Review your memory verse. Write it in a note to a friend or on Facebook.

DAY 3 & DAY 4

Entering Your Story

Broken Shalom

The story of the Bible tells us that shalom has been broken, and our stories also reveal this reality. When I am asked to tell my story, I almost always begin with, "When I was seven . . ."

> When I was seven, my parents got divorced. I don't remember the moment when my parents told us this was happening. I remember the days of frolicking in Fairlawn, the modern subdivision that promised hope for a new future to the adults and provided an idyllic childhood play place for the kids. Then I remember snow, winter, and leafless trees laced with ice . . . a dreary apartment complex in Atlanta, Georgia. I remember taking a bus an hour away to visit my father on the weekends. As a seven-year-old, all I really understood was that my life had drastically, suddenly, and violently been deconstructed. Shalom was vandalized.

As we learned in our first study, not all stories make sense—some feel more like puzzles with missing pieces. This particular story of shalom being shattered lacks crucial plot elements and connectives; it lives for me as fragments of scenes and settings. Point of view is skewed because it is only seen from my seven-year-old memory that clearly shut down in the shattering. It was cold and wintry when we moved, because it was January, but I am fairly certain the memory of snow comes from another year when we had a severe ice storm. Still, the sense of snow, cold, and death describes the feeling of that time well. As we remember stories of our worlds being wrecked, we must recognize that there may be more questions than answers in the memory. Read and answer the following questions to help you write and reflect on your story:

1. Reread Genesis 3:4–7. One of the reasons the fall occurred was because Eve wanted to know more so she could exert more control over her life. This desire for control is also one of the consequences of the fall (Gen. 3:16).

    a. Think about some areas of uncertainty in your life. How might knowing more bring you a greater sense of safety and security?

    b. What are some ways you have tried to control your life? How have they worked out?

   c. Ask God to meet you in your uncertainty and help you avoid turning to quick ways to find relief from your confusion or fear.

2. Tell a story of when shalom was disrupted in your life. Consider the following questions as you write the story:
   a. Did the disruption come from external circumstances beyond your control or from something you did?

   b. What beautiful creation was destroyed? Did you have the sense that nothing new could ever come out of the devastation?

Like Humpty Dumpty, we can't get up and dust ourselves off after the fall. All of mankind, including God's entire creation, is critically affected and utterly helpless to heal ourselves. Our fall from glory did not just create distance between us and God, but also depravity in our hearts. As a result of the fall, every aspect of our humanity, and God's creation, is in desperate need of restoration. All things are broken. And just as we should pay careful attention to a trustworthy doctor when pursuing a correct diagnosis, we can only discover the great degree to which something is broken by listening to God speak to us in the Bible.

—Scotty Smith and Steven Curtis Chapman, *Restoring Broken Things*

c. Did you try to achieve shalom/rest/security in your life apart from God?

d. How did the story end (if it has ended)?

DAY 5

- Review your memory verse. Say it aloud three times.

Living Story

Repentance and the Fall

We saw that Adam and Eve, when they discovered they were naked and felt shame, tried to cover themselves, hide from God, and blame one another. They compounded the first sin by further trying to save themselves.

When life is out of balance, we seek to restore order and harmony because we were made for intimacy, connection, and wholeness. If we believe that God is up in heaven reading the Sunday paper, distant, uninvolved, and unconcerned about our stories, we will seek to restore shalom on our own terms. This kind of seeking to make life work is the essence of what the Bible calls idolatry. Shopping, playing sports, drinking alcohol, working, keeping relationships, viewing pornography, cleaning the house—any of these can be idols we turn to for security and significance, or to numb the pain of wounding we experienced.

I encourage you to spend some time reflecting and praying on this section. Be honest with God and with yourself. Some of your answers may be ones you don't wish to share with the entire group. Perhaps you want to share them privately with a trusted friend or a leader.

1. Search for some of the chief idols in your life:

    a. Write down some places, people, things, or activities that provide a temporary sense of relief or significance.

    b. Which ones do you think might have become idols that you trust in to save you from the struggles of living in a fallen world?

Repentance, as we learned in chapter 1, results from hunger. When we recognize that the idols we have chosen can never cover the shame or heal the ache, we turn to God and cry, "Save me!" The Holy Spirit helps us to cry out.

2. What might repentance look like regarding some of the ways you have tried to manage your life apart from God? Check any that might apply and comment:

☐ Taking one Sunday off every month from volunteering in the church nursery.

☐ Finding and attending a recovery group for a specific addiction.

☐ Cutting your time spent on Facebook or any other social media by two-thirds.

- ☐ Lovingly telling your spouse that he/she cannot speak to you in that angry, demeaning tone of voice.

- ☐ Lovingly apologizing to your friends and family for the ways you have demanded that they fill your need for approval.

- ☐ Saying something kind about an enemy instead of making a slighting comment.

- ☐ Write your own:

PRAYING STORY

A Prayer about Fallen Stories and Broken Shalom

Dear Lord, we come to you with broken hearts over broken stories. We are confused and hurt about why you have allowed our daughter to turn away from us, our husband to be distant, our friend to turn on us, our job to be taken. Our sin nature makes us want to rebel and find a way to live apart from you.

But that's not really what we want. What we really want is you, dear Lord. We cry to you, we ask you, we beg you, to meet us in the midst of our broken shalom. You don't have to fix it, just bring us your presence in a way that we will rest in your arms, trusting in you and waiting for you to redeem in your way and your time, not ours.

Psalms to pray: Psalms 38, 39, and 55

Moving Forward

We are compulsive sinners, but the good news of the gospel tells us we are liberated from the enslaving power of sin! It is essential to remember and tell our stories of rescue and redemption as a way of continuing to grow in faith, hope, and love. In the next study we will have an opportunity to remember, write, and share these stories.

4

Story Feasting: An Interlude

KEY THEMES:

- We are all called to tell the stories of God's wonderful goodness.
- Sharing our stories is essential to growing in faith, hope, and love because it helps us remember redemption and focus on our future hope.

DAY 1

A friend from seminary had been struggling with disunity among church board members. I had told him about "story feasting," and he decided to try his version of it.

> At the next meeting, he announced to the group that there would be no minutes nor motions taken that evening. Instead, each man would have twenty minutes to find a quiet place and write a story of rescue. Then they would return to tell these stories. For the first time in one of these meetings there was complete

silence. The men just stared at my preacher friend, who smiled, handed them the assignment, and sent them off.

Twenty minutes later, they returned. William, at eighty one, an original board member, and one of the wisest and gentlest, spoke first. He had tears in his eyes as he thanked the pastor for reminding him that he was a redeemed man. He went on to tell the story of how he became a Christian during World War II.

Rod, the youngest elder who had settled in a strict, conservative camp where there was little room for the gospel to breathe in any of the hot-button issues, softened as he heard William's story. For the first time in a while, he thought of his deceased grandfather who had led him to faith. His grandfather had been a kind and gentle man with a homegrown Christianity. As Rod had begun studying theology, he found himself silently critiquing his grandfather's simple understandings. Listening to William, a man from his grandfather's era, Rod began to realize both his own arrogance in criticizing his grandfather and the arrogance with which he sometimes approached his work on the board.

At that moment, Rod decided to tell a different story than he had written. He told a rescue story of being raised in a home ravaged by an alcoholic father and of a grandfather who cared for him. Early on hot summer mornings, his grandfather would come calling at his house and together they would walk to the nearby pond and fish for bream with cane poles. As they waited for fish and swatted flies and mosquitoes, his grandfather would tell him about the fisher of men who loved him and died for him. Though they never caught many fish, it was in these times that Rod's heart was deeply hooked by his grandfather's beloved fisher of men.

From there, the stories took off. Before long, at least four of the thirteen men in the room had tears in their eyes as waves of understanding washed over them. With each story, each man was again reminded of his own rescue story. Each knew that a

---

Shared stories are not easily walked away from.

—Daniel Taylor, *The Healing Power of Stories*

loving God had pursued him to the ends of the earth. A gospel shift occurred on the board that evening, as many men came to grips with their sinner-saint status.

The History of Feasting

We are learning about the grand narrative of Scripture, the story of grace God is telling in the cosmos and in our lives. But as we discovered in our study of Psalm 78, we must do more than learn the story–we must share it!

Sharing our stories is essential to growing in faith, hope, and love. As we hear the stories others tell of how God has worked redemption in their lives, we often remember marvelous deeds God has done in our own lives. In telling stories of wrecked shalom, the Spirit often moves to grow our hope so we can say, "This will make a really good story one day." Listening to others' stories draws us to know and love them in new ways. Sharing our own stories is a gift of love to other people.

"Okay," you may say, "I get why I need to share my story. But what's the deal with a feast?" The theme of feasting runs throughout God's story. God called his people to gather at appointed times to remember redemption and rescue in their lives. Everyone in the community participated in these feasts, the very young and the very old, the marginalized aliens and the community leaders. Traditional foods were an essential part of the feast: meat, bread, and wine were offered and enjoyed in thanksgiving to God.

In the Old Testament, the feast of Passover celebrated God's rescue of the Israelites from slavery in Egypt. In the New Testament, the Passover feast takes a strange turn when Christ says, "I tell you the truth, unless you eat the flesh of the Son of Man and drink his blood, you have no life in you. Whoever eats my flesh and drinks my blood has eternal life, and I will raise him up at the last day" (John 6:53–54). Now we remember the ultimate rescue as we feast regularly on Christ's body and blood in the sacrament of Holy Communion.

As followers of Christ, we gather to offer our own stories to God and our community, naming both the tragedy and redemption of our narratives. Sharing our stories and hearing others' stories strengthens our faith, increases our hope, and compels us to move into a hurting world with love. Story feasting deepens the bonds of community and propels the mission of love that marks us as Christians.

Unlike the men on my friend's board, you have a week to prepare for your story feast. Walk through the preparatory questions and get ready for the best feast you've ever experienced!

DAY 2

Food for the Feast

Feasts involve special foods. It may be a favorite treat you enjoy from the grocery store (double chocolate fudge chunk ice cream, anyone?), or it could be your dad's special barbecued rib recipe.

1. What "ritual food" will you share at the feast? What significance does it have for you?

It is important to tell at least from time to time the secret of who we truly and fully are—even if we tell it only to ourselves—because otherwise we run the risk of losing track of who we truly and fully are and little by little come to accept the highly edited version we put forth in hope that the world will find it more acceptable than the real thing. . . . Finally, I suspect that it is by entering the deep place inside us where our secrets are kept that we come perhaps closer than we do anywhere else to the One who, whether we realize it or not, is of all our secrets the most telling and the most precious we have to tell.

—Frederick Buechner, *Telling Secrets*

Ground Rules

All feasts are governed by convention. Rules for story feasts help to assure a safe and welcoming environment. The following five suggestions should help build a foundation:

Tell your story purposefully. The main purpose of this story feast is to glorify God. Recognize that all sorts of stories glorify God in many different ways. This core purpose does not mean our stories have to be overly spiritual!

2. Think of a story that you like to tell. How might it draw others to see the beauty, majesty, humor, holiness, strength, kindness, or any other characteristic of God?

Tell your story honestly. Telling a story honestly means being willing to examine our own hearts. We have to open our hearts to hear what God and others have to say to us through the telling of the story. Ask the Holy Spirit to reveal more about who God is, who others are, or who you are in the telling of the story.

Tell your story honorably. Avoid the temptation toward gossip, slander, or vengeance in your stories. Don't avoid telling the truth or pretend that something cruel did not hurt you. Here is an example: I want to honor my parents always, but the reality is that their decision to divorce caused deep pain in my life. As long as I tell how I felt and don't stray to the topic of their mistakes or sinfulness, I am honoring my story and them. I may also tell a story publicly differently than I would tell it to my spouse, a trusted friend, or counselor.

3. Think of a story of being harmed by someone. How could you tell that story honorably?

Listen to stories with integrity. We should attend seriously to others' stories. We should be willing to engage and always honor the privacy of the storyteller.

4. Have you experienced being listened to with integrity? What did the listener do to make you feel honored?

Take part. No one is required to tell a story (though it will be fairly dull if no one does). You are welcome to come and listen without the intent of sharing a story. But keep an open heart, because people often remember their own stories when they hear the stories of others.

DAY 3

Prepare the story

Write the story.

1. Reread the story questions in the *Engaging Your Story* section of each chapter.

2. Reread the stories you have written to respond to those questions. Choose one that you would like to work on more and to share with the group.

3. Write it out if you haven't already.

DAY 4

Reflect on the story

Consider any or all of the following questions:

1. What does this story reveal about you or others? What does it reflect about your style of relating to others?

2. What does this story show about who God is and what he has done?

3. Is there anything about the events of the story that makes you question the goodness of the heart of God? If so, take those questions to him in prayer. Review Psalm 77 for an excellent example of a psalmist crying out to God in confusion over the events of his life and the resultant reaffirmation of his faith.

4. What does the story reveal about sin, grace, or redemption?

5. Take your story to his story–the Word of God. Is there a story in the Bible that reminds you of yours? A character? A Psalm?

DAY 5

Edit the story

1. After reflecting on the above questions, rewrite where necessary.
   a. Take out details that aren't essential to the key point of the story.
   b. Add in details that would make the story clearer.

Share the story

2. Each group member will be allotted about ten minutes for telling their story and hearing the thoughts of others. You can read a story you have written or you can tell the story from memory or using an outline.
   a. Would you like to read or tell your story?
   b. If you are going to read the story, remember to engage your audience. Look at them and read it to them, expecting them to respond.
   c. If you are going to tell the story, make sure you have the key points outlined. You've only got ten minutes, so it's important to focus on the essentials. Practice telling the story beforehand to see how long it takes.

When we haven't the time to listen to each other's stories we seek out experts to tell us how to live.

—Dr. Rachel Remen, *Kitchen-Table Wisdom*

Finally the Feast

Ideally, you should feast for about two and a half hours:

30 minutes: Feast and fellowship.

10 minutes: Leader introduces story theme and prays.

90 minutes (maximum): Story sharing. Ten minutes per person, so if your group is larger than ten people, divide into two smaller groups.

15 minutes: Close with a time of prayer for one another's stories.

DAY 6

Revisit the story

Note: In this chapter, just this once, you have an extra day to follow up after the feast. Think through the following questions and jot some notes before the next meeting.

Revise the story. Consider the process of telling the story.

1. What kinds of responses did the group give you about your story?

2. How did you feel as you told your story?

3. Did you notice anything new about your story through the telling or through a group member's response?

4. Write down any specific prayers you will pray for other group members based on the stories you heard.

5

Redemption: Restoring Shalom

KEY THEMES:

- Redemption means that we are freed from living as sin slaves. We are raised with Christ to live a life of free and glorious worship.
- Redemption is the part of the story when shalom is partially restored. We await the day when shalom will be finally and fully restored.

DAY 1

The caller ID revealed it was my husband. It was 8:30 a.m. on a Monday morning. Kip rarely called until lunchtime unless there was a schedule change. His terse "Hi . . ." that returned my flat "Good morning" told me it was no good morning for him. "Guess what?" he asked. I waited for the bad news. "The roof of the surgical center collapsed; we can't use eight operating rooms." He went on to tell me that during morning rounds he had seen a patient who had fallen off the wagon, literally stumbling from a platform in a drunken stupor after being sober for ten years. Kip would have to stay late to operate on the man's shattered femur.

I knew he had called to hear reassurance from his wife, of harmony on the home front, of a world where money was not draining away rapidly and people were not destroying their lives stupidly, but I had no good news to report. The kids were fighting in the background as they tackled the task of cleaning the kitchen; I was trying to escape but had discovered my vehicle had a dead battery. We were both self-consumed and unable to offer comfort and hope to the other. Life was broken, and we desperately needed to know the Restorer of broken things.

This is where we left the story in chapter 3, with the entire cosmos and all relationships deeply broken by sin. Thankfully, as we said before, the story doesn't end there. This chapter explores Christ's work of redemption, which is the beginning of a story that concludes with the full and final righting of all things.

Engaging Scripture: Genesis 3 and 2 Corinthians 5

Background

Genre. (For Genesis 3, see chapter 3.) 2 Corinthians is an epistle. This word simply means, "letter." In the days before texting, email, Facebook, and cell phones, letters were frequently written to convey important messages.

The coming of the kingdom of God represents a final state of cosmic redemption, in which God and God's creatures dwell together in harmony, righteousness, and delight. In fact, "the coming of the kingdom of God" is just the New Testament way of spelling shalom.

—Cornelius Plantinga, *Engaging God's World: A Christian Vision of Faith, Learning, and Living*

Context. This book is the second of Paul's letters written to the church at Corinth. In this letter, Paul responds to opponents who have questioned his ministry and motives. He explains that his story and ministry are inseparable.

Redemption: Freed to Worship

As we saw in our study of the fall, God previews the chapter on redemption even as he addresses Satan in the garden (Gen. 3:15). The story of redemption continues to unfold throughout the Old Testament and into the New Testament.

The Gospels, Matthew, Mark, Luke, and John, tell the true story of the life of the main character in redemption: Jesus. The word *gospel* is from the Greek *euangelion*, which means "message of good news." In ancient times, after a conquering king defeated the enemy, a herald would announce the good news that a new king had arrived to bring peace and hope.

The Gospels of Jesus Christ tell this part of the story: Jesus is the King who defeated the enemy, evil, once and for all, in his life, death, and resurrection. In doing so, he redeemed his people. He liberated us from a life of slavery to sin, so we can live a full and free life worshipping and serving in God's kingdom.

Read Genesis 3 and 2 Corinthians 5:14–21. Choose a verse you would like to memorize for this particular study. Find one

---

It is the gospel that continues to remind us that our day-to-day acceptance with the Father is not based on what we do for God but upon what Christ did for us in his sinless life and sin-bearing death. I began to see that we stand before God today as righteous as we ever will be, even in heaven, because he has clothed us with the righteousness of his Son. Therefore, I don't have to perform to be accepted by God. Now I am free to obey him and serve him because I am already accepted in Christ (see Rom. 8:1). My driving motivation now is not guilt but gratitude.

—Jerry Bridges, "Gospel-Driven Sanctification"

that feels personal to you and your story. Write it here or on a note card or a sticky note.

DAY 2

Redemption brings stunning transformation for the believer and the cosmos. To help us recognize and remember some of the effects of redemption, let's think about the four *re*'s.

- Review your memory verse. Write it here.

1. Re-location:

   a. How does God's question to Adam invite him to "re-locate" (Gen. 3:9)? Where is he? Where does God want him to be? Have you ever experienced God calling you out of hiding?

b. How is God's re-location of Adam and Eve an act of kindness and provision (Gen. 3: 22–24)?

2. Re-situation:

The fall, as we saw, changed the situation, or the state of affairs, of creation. For this moment in the story, it appears that Satan has the upper hand.

a. How does God make clear that evil has not won (Gen. 3:15)?

b. After the fall, Adam and Eve are newly aware and now ashamed of their nakedness. How does God "re-situate" them? In what way is this re-situation an act of kindness (Gen. 3:21–24)?

Theological Themes: Imputed Righteousness and Justification

Christ's redemption brings us fallen sinners into a new legal state. Two theological terms used to define this state are *justification* and *imputed righteousness*. Both of these terms describe what 2 Corinthians 5:21 means when it says, "God made him who had no sin to be sin for us, so that in him we might become the righteousness of God."

The death of Christ had two major legal ramifications. The first is that we were legally declared not guilty by God, the only judge. The reality is we are guilty of sin, so how did God declare us not guilty? Christ became sin and died. When we accept Christ's death as the payment for our sins, we are justified because God has accepted Christ's payment as a substitute for what we owe. Wow! What love is this that the Father has bestowed upon us! No other god would ever die for humans. It is an amazing story—and all the more, because it's true!

The second major legal ramification is even more stunning. Not only did God declare us not guilty, but he gave us a new status: righteousness. This righteousness is imputed to us, that is, we are judged as "right," so that we will never have to go through another trial for our sins. When Christ paid for our sins, he did so for all sins, past and present. This is why as redeemed sinners we are free! The fact that righteousness has been imputed to us doesn't mean we will never sin again, but it does mean that our sin will never be counted against us again. Romans 7 says we will continue to struggle with sin until Christ has fully established his kingdom on the final day, but Romans 8 asserts that we can never be condemned and tried for these sins if we have trusted in Christ's death for our legal status of righteousness. It's another puzzling story Scripture tells, but it is truly great news!

DAY 3

1. Re-conciliation:

As we saw in chapter 3, the major impact of the fall was to divide what was meant to be united. Adam and Eve were alienated from one another and alienated from God. Listen to 2 Corinthians 5:19–20 as translated in *The Message*:

> All this comes from the God who settled the relationship between us and him, and then called us to settle our relationships with each other. God put the world square with himself through the Messiah, giving the world a fresh start by offering forgiveness of sins. God has given us the task of telling everyone what he is doing. We're Christ's representatives. God uses us to persuade men and women to drop their differences and enter into God's work of making things right between them. We're speaking for Christ himself now: Become friends with God; he's already a friend with you.

   a. What impact did redemption have on God's relationship with us and our relationship with one another?

b. What did God offer the world?

c. What are we supposed to do since we have been reconciled with God?

2. Re-creation:

In the fall, every good created thing was destroyed and despoiled by sin.

a. What happens to those who trust in Christ's life, death, and resurrection to save us from slavery to sin? "Now we look inside, and what we see is that anyone united with the Messiah gets a fresh start, is created new. The old life is gone; a new life burgeons! Look at it!" (2 Cor. 5:14 MSG)

b. As new creations in Christ, what are we called to do (2 Cor. 5:15, 18–20)?

If redemption justifies us and makes us righteous, you might ask, "Why do we still sin?" Romans 7 explains that while our truest selves have been transformed by Christ's redemption, and we live free of the condemning effects of the law, we will continue to struggle with sin until the day of full restoration. It is important to remember that by our own strength we are powerless to defeat sin. We must rely on the Holy Spirit and believe in the reality that we truly own the status of righteousness in Christ.

- Review your memory verse. Post it on Facebook or write it in a note to a friend.

The most basic categories present in the gospel are creation, fall, and redemption. Jesus' announcement declares a resounding "yes" to his good creation and at the same time a definitive "no" to the sin that has defiled it. The gospel is about the restoration and renewal of the creation from sin. In the history of the Western church redemption has often been misunderstood to be salvation from the creation rather than salvation of the creation. In the proclamation of the gospel Jesus announces that he is liberating the good creation from the power of sin.

—Michael Goheen, "Reading the Bible as One Story"

DAY 4

Entering Your Story

Christ's redemption does not simply restore creation to its original condition–it renews it. Christ takes what is broken and makes it better than it was before it was broken.

Redemption Story

Imagine a forty-three-year-old woman who undergoes rotator cuff surgery to heal a shoulder battered by years of awkward serving of a tennis ball. The skilled and gifted orthopedic surgeon works his scalpel magic with magnificent results. She hopes to have a stronger shoulder that will, with arduous physical therapy, ultimately allow her to play tennis again. Imagine her stunned surprise when she emerges from surgery with a new arm, muscled and toned like Venus Williams's and free to swing with power and grace. This small picture hints at the restoration and renewal that Jesus effects for us in redemption. Choose one of the following topics to write a redemption story:

1. Think of a "hampered shoulder" in your life. Tell of a time when a dream had been shattered, when there was something severely broken in your life and you saw beauty restored.

2. Tell of a time when you needed rescue or redemption and you were saved. What was the situation you needed saving from? What rescue came? Who were the characters involved? Can you see God working in any way in this story?

DAY 5

- Review your memory verse. Say it aloud three times.

Living Story

1. Because we have been reconciled to God through redemption, we live with the hope of reconciliation for all of our broken relationships.

    a. Write down one broken relationship where you would like to see redemption.

b. Write down three things you can do to begin the movement toward reconciliation. Remember, we are not called to be reconciled to an unrepentant sinner. However, we are called to forgive, which involves praying for an unrepentant sinner and hoping that their hearts will change.

PRAYING STORY

2. Read the quote from *Restoring Broken Things.* Do you see yourself more as a rosebud that was diseased and is now being healed, or as a rosebud whose petals have been

---

The Redemption we receive through the work of Jesus will enable us to realize the potential contained in Creation—which will only be fully realized at Consummation! Think of a magnificent rose bud (Creation) that became diseased (Fall) but is being healed (Redemption) and will one day reach full blossom (Consummation).

—Scotty Smith and Steven Curtis Chapman *Restoring Broken Things*

torn off and thrown on the ground? Write a prayer to God about where you are in believing the full effects of redemption on your life.

3. A prayer for all of us:

Oh Lord, show us your story of grace written in our lives. Help us to see the whole places and the broken places. Help us to see redemption where there may seem to be none. Help us to acknowledge where we have tried to find our own way to make our worlds work by trusting in idols. Most of all, help us know how deeply forgiven and loved we are by you.

Moving Forward

As those who have chosen to follow Christ the King, we have faith based on the memory of his rescue and redemption in our lives. We also live with great hope because we know the end of the story: shalom will one day be fully and finally restored.

6

Consummation: Shalom Reigns

KEY THEMES:

- Remembering the future of our story, the return and ultimate reign of shalom for eternity, bolsters our hope in the present.
- Jesus is already making all things new, and he calls and empowers us to join him in kingdom restoration.

DAY 1

The due date for my first son came and went without him making his exit from my womb. Concerned friends and family called me every day to see if there were any signs of labor. I thanked them for their call and inwardly seethed—not because I was angry with them but because I had long ago lost patience with pregnancy. As days went on, I began to wonder if this child would live inside of me until he was a teenager (remember, hugely pregnant women, especially in the South in August, are not the most rational creatures). But one verse reminded me of my hope: "And I am certain that God, who began the good work within you, will continue his work until it is finally finished on that day when Jesus Christ returns" (Phil.1:6 NLT).

As I waited in the hope that my son would be born before the second coming, the verse reminded me that God does not begin a work and then grow weary of it and wander off. As believers, we hope with the entire cosmos for the new creation to reach full term.

The final chapter of the grand narrative, told in Revelation 21 and 22, is often called *consummation.* This word derives from Latin roots for "summing up" and is defined by Webster's Dictionary as "complete in every detail; perfect." The new heaven and new earth is the ultimate completion of what God began. This ending far surpasses any we have experienced or dreamed in this life. Not only is everything set right, it is set more than right: shalom reigns forever. This is the ongoing story that is meant to consume our lives, both now and for eternity.

Engaging Scripture: Revelation 1, 21-22

Background

Genre. Apocalypse: Generally speaking, *apocalypse,* a common theme in Hollywood movies, narrates end time events and often involves epic battles between good and evil. The

---

In speaking of Jesus, Isaiah said, "Of the increase of his government and peace [shalom] there will be no end" (Isaiah 9:7). Jesus' peaceful kingdom is increasing incrementally and will be so until the consummation of the fullness of his kingdom.

—Scotty Smith, *The Reign of Grace*

word *revelation* in Greek is "apokalypsis" and means literally "to uncover." The first verse of Revelation tells us what it is about: "the revelation of Jesus Christ." Revelation is always about knowing who Christ is and the hope he brings into stories of darkness.

As Eugene Peterson comments, many people do not want to read Revelation on its own terms. To help us understand what Revelation is about, let's begin at the beginning.

1. Read Revelation 1, 21 and 22. Choose a verse you would like to memorize for this particular study. Find one that feels personal to you and your story. Write it here, on a note card, or a sticky note.

The Revelation both forces and enables me to look at what is spread out right before me, and to see it with fresh eyes. It forces me because, being the last book in the Bible, I cannot finish the story apart from it. It enables me because, by using the unfamiliar language of apocalyptic vision, my imagination is called into vigorous play. In spite of these obvious benefits and necessary renewals, there are many people who stubbornly refuse to read it, or (which is just as bad) refuse to read it on its own terms.

—Eugene Peterson, *Reversed Thunder*

2. Let's take a close look at the introduction to the book, Revelation 1:1.

   a. What is being uncovered in the book of Revelation (v. 1:1a)? Have you ever had a moment when an important truth was revealed to you? What was it like when something previously hidden became uncovered?

   b. Who is Revelation about? Who is doing the revealing? If you were nearby when Jesus revealed himself and began to tell you his story, what would you want to know about him?

c. What is the purpose of the revelation?

DAY 2

Many people treat the book of Revelation as a predictive prophecy about something that will happen in the far-off future. In reality, it is a predictive prophecy about something that has already begun and will have its ultimate fulfillment in the future. As you look at the cosmos and your story, do you see signs that restoration has already begun?

Revelation 21 and 22 tell of a second creation, not a return to Eden, but a beginning of a brand-new story where shalom will surpass anything ever known and will last eternally.

- Review memory verse. Write it on Facebook or in a note to a friend.

We must always keep focused on the gospel because it is in the nature of sanctification that as we grow, we see more and more of our sinfulness. Instead of driving us to discouragement, though, this should drive us to the gospel. It is the gospel believed every day that is the only enduring motivation to pursue progressive sanctification even in those times when we don't seem to see progress. That is why I use the expression "gospel-driven sanctification" and that is why we need to "preach the gospel to ourselves every day."

—Jerry Bridges, "Gospel-Driven Sanctification"

Theological Theme: Sanctification and Glorification

Sanctification is a big word that refers to the ongoing process of the renewal of our hearts and minds. In this process, which occurs after we have been justified, our false self, the natural bent toward sin, is transformed into our true self, a mind and heart that reflects the image of Christ. The Westminster Shorter Catechism (Q.35), defines sanctification as "the work of God's free grace, whereby we are renewed in the whole man after the image of God, and are enabled more and more to die unto sin, and live unto righteousness."

As we read the description of the new heavens and new earth life, we understand what this change will be like when it is completed. Consummation brings glorification. As Scotty Smith explains, sanctification is a "progressive change in our nature." In glorification, at the second coming of Jesus, "justified sinners are instantaneously made to be perfectly righteous, like Jesus. Every violation of shalom will be redeemed."*

Shalom fully restored means there will be perfect harmony. No longer will we be divided by differences; no longer will we be despoiled by selfish demands. We won't murder our friends or family with mean words. We won't be tired by our exhaustive efforts to please people. We won't be torn by our desire to be known and our fear of being known.

At the end of the story, when sanctification is completed in glorification, we will begin a new and unending story of living as we were created to live. We will love to be loved and we will love to love. We will be like Jesus, for we will see him clearly, face to face. We will surrender ourselves utterly and completely to the joy of worshipping God. We will sing and speak with a heart that overflows with delight in God and delight in his glorious creation.

The good news is that we don't have to wait for Christ's return to live this life. Shalom restoration, as we saw in the last chapter, has begun—on this earth and in our hearts. Christ is making all things new now, so let us rejoice in this process of transformation that is taking place in us this very moment. Even if we can't see it or feel it, it is true. We are being renewed and restored, and one day we will be finished in the consummation of his glory, which is the end and the beginning of our truest story.

* Scotty Smith, *The Reign of Grace: The Delights and Demands of God's Love* (West Monroe, LA: Howard Publishing, 2003), 56.

DAY 3

1. Read Genesis 1 and 2 and Revelation 21 and 22 in one sitting if possible.
   a. Write down three things you notice about the creation in Genesis 1 and 2.

   b. Write down three things you notice about the new heavens and the new earth.

c. What similarities do you notice between the first heavens and the first earth in Genesis and the new heavens and new earth in Revelation? What differences do you notice?

2. Revelation 21:5: "Behold, I am making all things new" (ESV). Let's take some of the pieces of this verse and chew on them slowly.

    a. *Behold* means "Check this out–it is awe-some, worship-worthy!" Read the description of the new heavens and new earth in Revelation 21-22. What things would you like to "check out" or "behold"?

b. *New*: The word in Greek, *kaina*, means "new, unheard of, the latest thing." It is like saying, "now for something really different!" What things about the new heavens and new earth are unheard of, really different (Rev. 21:1–5)?

c. *Making*: The Greek word translated "making" is *poieo*, from which we derive the word *poem*. How do you see the creation of the new heavens and new earth as an act of poetry? What acts of poetic, imaginative, beyond-belief creating do you think Jesus is doing in your life by the power of the Holy Spirit?

DAY 4

ENTERING YOUR STORY

In the movie *The Passion,* Jesus addresses his mother, Mary, from the cross, saying, "Behold I make all things new." Take on the role of Mary for a moment. Imagine what she might have felt watching her son, the Messiah, die on a cross.

Jesus' words, though not spoken from the cross as the movie depicts, are spoken to us all in the moments of watching our dreams die and seeing our stories shattered before our eyes. But we have the privilege of knowing what Mary did not in that moment. As Jesus' body was being broken for sinners on the cross, he was beginning the process of making all things new. Because we know the narrative ends with shalom reigning for eternity, we can look at a the most dismal or dire circumstances and say, "This will make a really good story one day."

A Consummation-Anticipation Story

As I am writing this, the country of Haiti has suffered a devastating earthquake that will likely cause the country to implode. I weep for young missionary friends who recently opened an orphanage to minister to the broken families of Haiti. Though their orphanage is undamaged, they need to leave the country for the safety of the orphans and themselves. In times such as these, it is truly hard to say, "This will make a really good story one day." But Revelation tells us that God will not only restore but will renew Haiti. As hard as it is to believe, one day there will be no more broken buildings, no more crime, and no more orphans in Haiti. Because of that true and lovely ending to the story, we continue to dream of and work for restoration *now.*

1. Think of a story where shalom is broken right now. It can be personal or it can be systemic (like education, health

care, sex slave trade, etc.). Write an imaginative story of what this broken story or system will look like in the new heavens and new earth.

2. Our stories do reach resolution along the way. Sometimes the resolution is not what we would have hoped for (cancer takes our friend's life; our parents don't get back together). Other times it brings a happy ending (we finally land the job we have dreamed of; a relationship with a friend is restored). Write the story of one happy

ending in your life. What did it feel like? How did it give you a small foretaste of the shalom you will experience in eternity?

DAY 5

- Review memory verse. Write it on Facebook or in a note to a friend.

Begin thinking and praying about a plan for restoring broken things. Discuss this with your group when you meet.

Living Story

As a group or as individuals, choose a broken place in your world or beyond your world: a neighborhood, a relationship, orphans, poverty, a school . . . the list goes on. Think of one thing you can do to be a part of the process of restoration of shalom in that place. Write down a specific plan with a date to be completed.

1. What would you like to do?

2. List organizations or people you could contact:

Our duty is to help the natural creation, in anticipation of its final, glorious rebirth. We are to keep our charge as responsible managers, as stewards, and strive to live in a way that refrains from extending humanity's abuse of nature and instead looks for ways to reverse it.

—Nathan Bierma, *Bringing Heaven down to Earth*

3. Write a target date for contacting them:

4. Write a target date for doing the work:

Praying Story

Pray this restoration prayer:

Dear Creator and Restorer of all broken things, how we long for the day when there will be no more death, disease, destruction, or despoiling in our world. How we long for the day when we will always be with you and you will always be with us! We can't even imagine what that will be like. But even as we long for that day, we thank you that your restoration and redemption work has already begun. Thank you for the glimpses we see, the foretastes we savor, and the rumors we hear of your work being done. Draw us to live with kingdom joy in the hope of the new heavens and new earth coming. Show us our assigned realms and the restoration projects you want us to take part in until that day comes. In the name of your Son the Redeemer and by the power of the Holy Spirit, we ask these things. Amen!

Moving Forward

Indeed, we pray such prayers of hope because we know the end of God's grand narrative of grace, and it is a really good one. As we come near the end of our story together, we must gather for one last feast, a foretaste of the feasts of worship and remembrance we will one day celebrate eternally.

7

Finally Feasting

KEY THEMES:

- Life in a fallen and redeemed world brings the tension of living with heartache and hope.
- When Christ returns, our stories will no longer be tainted with the fall. Until then, we tell our stories as a way to remember God's rescue and dream of the day when there will be no more pain, death, sorrow, or sickness.

DAY 1

We have spent a sweet season learning the story of the gospel. God created us with dignity and purpose. God called us to worship and delight in him by being fruitful, multiplying, and stewarding the earth. Shalom was shattered by our sin, but the story did not end there. Because God loves us, he made a way for us to be reconciled, redeemed, restored, and renewed by his mercy and grace. As redeemed sinners, we have a kingdom call: to learn, live, and love in this story of grace that God has written in us, even as we await the final and full restoration of all broken shalom.

This is the grand narrative Scripture tells. Our author God did not stop with writing his love in Scripture; he has etched his grace uniquely into each of our individual stories. These are the stories we celebrate. As we await the final feast in the new heavens and the new earth, we gather to remember our stories now. Remembering takes us through the terrain of tragedy and the hinterlands of heartache but thankfully does not leave us there. On every moment of wrecked shalom, God has stamped his mark of rescue and redemption. In this final feast for now, you'll have an opportunity to walk through a *whole* story, to see with others the marvelous works God has done, is doing, and will do in your life.

Story Feast Review

Review the instructions and ground rules for a story feast in chapter 4.

Plan your feasting food

Feasts involve special foods. It may be a favorite treat you enjoy from the grocery store, or it could be your grandmother's banana pudding. What "ritual food" will you share at the feast? What significance does it have for you?

The journey homewards. Coming home. That's what it's all about. The journey to the coming of the Kingdom. That's probably the chief difference between the Christian and the secular artist—the purpose of the work, be it story or music or painting, is to further the coming of the kingdom, to make us aware of our status as children of God, and to turn our feet toward home.

—Madeleine L'Engle, *Walking on Water: Reflections on Faith and Art*

DAY 2

Prepare the story

Use the chart and the following questions to help you consider the story you will write in the coming days. Make some notes for use when you write your story.

1. Shalom: Tell of a time in your story when things were "the way they were supposed to be." Look for harmony, peace, "the world working," intimacy, etc.

2. Fall: How was the shalom wrecked in that story? What occurred to break the harmony? What legitimate longings did you experience?

Creation/Shalom	Fall/Shalom Wrecked	 Redemption/Restoring Shalom	Consummation/ Shalom Reigns
		Faith, Hope, & Love Grow	
Genesis 1–2	Genesis 3	Gen. 3:9; 2 Cor. 5	
• Dignity, delight, difference, dominion • "The way it's supposed to be" • Worshipping Creator God by living in faith, hope, and love	• Distanced, despoiled • Sin spreads • Faith, hope, and love destroyed • Trust in idols, not God	• Reconciled to God through Christ • "Re-created": new creation • Redeemed: freed from sin to live for Christ	• New heavens; new earth • All broken things restored: no more death, disease, disappointment, distance • Unbroken worship: living a life of faith, hope, and love FOREVER

3. The fall compounded/sin replicating: Did you look to other idols to give you a sense of peace, security, and significance? What failures of faith, hope, and love did you experience?

4. Redemption: Do you see ways that God pursued and redeemed you in the fall? What kinds of "re-creation" (new life) did you experience? Did he rescue in the way you might have expected or wished? How did you see faith, hope, and love grow? (Think of passions, calling, or sense of mission).

5. Consummation: Obviously we don't know this part of the story yet. But we can imagine. Think of the particular story you discussed and imagine what that situation might be like in the new heavens and new earth, when our King, Jesus, has restored all broken things.

DAY 3

Write the story.

1. Review the "Engaging Your Story" sections of each chapter to find a story you would like to work with.

2. Choose one story and write it out, using the questions above and the story chart as your guide.

(Continued from previous page)

DAY 4

Reflect on the story.

1. What does this story reveal about you or about others? What does it reflect about your style of relating to others?

2. What does this story show about who God is and what he has done?

3. Is there anything about the events of the story that makes you question the goodness of the heart of God? If so, take those questions to him in prayer. Review Psalm 77 for an excellent example of a psalmist crying out to God in confusion over the events of his life and the resultant reaffirmation of his faith.

4. What does the story reveal about sin, grace, and redemption?

5. Take your story to Scripture. Is there a story in the Bible that reminds you of yours? A character? A psalm?

DAY 5

Edit the story.

1. After reflecting on the above questions, rewrite it if necessary.

2. Take out details that aren't essential to the key point of the story.

3. Add in details that would make the story clearer.

Share the story

Each group member will be allotted about ten minutes for telling the story and hearing the thoughts of others. You can read a story you have written or you can tell the story from your memory and an outline.

1. Would you like to read your story or tell it?

2. If you are going to read the story, remember to engage your audience. Look at them and read it to them, expecting them to respond.

3. If you are going to tell the story, make sure you have the key points outlined. You only have ten minutes, so it's important to focus on the essentials. Practice telling the story beforehand to see how long it takes.

Finally the Feast

Ideally, you should feast for about two and a half hours:

- 30 minutes: Feast and fellowship.
- 10 minutes: Leader introduces feast and prays.
- 90 minutes (maximum): Story sharing. Ten minutes per person, so if your group has nine or more people, divide into two smaller groups.
- 15 minutes: Close with a time of prayer for one another's stories.

EPILOGUE

Good stories have satisfying endings. And God's story of grace ends with the beginning of an eternal life of worship. To wrap this study up in a way that leads you to carry on into the future, I encourage you to look back, to remember, to grieve, and to celebrate the contours of the terrain you have walked.

DAY 1

Flip back through the study. Find your memory verses.

1. Write them all here or perhaps in a separate place where you can revisit them often.

2. Are there any stories in your life related to the verses? Write at least the titles of the stories or the whole story if you have time.

Don't adventures ever have an end? I suppose not. Someone else always has to carry on the story.

—J.R.R. Tolkien, *The Fellowship of the Ring*

DAY 2

Revise your story from the final story feast. Consider the process of telling the story.

1. What kinds of responses did the group give you about your story?

2. How did you feel as you told your story?

3. Did you notice anything new about your story through the telling or through a group member's response?

DAY 3 & DAY 4

Write down any specific prayers you will pray for other group members based on the stories you heard.

DAY 5

Finish the story. Write down some reflections on what you have learned over the course of this study and how it affects the way you live and love in God's story of grace.

There is more ahead as we carry on the story. Living in the tension between Christ's first coming and his second, we struggle daily with living in faith, hope, and love. Future *Living Story* studies will take us into the grand narrative of Scripture to explore how to:

- Surrender in faith to the God who does not always write our stories the way we would like
- Keep hoping when the story really does seem to be over, and it appears the bad guys have won
- Love in a way that connects us to the heart of God for a broken world that desperately needs to know and believe this story of love

As we part, I urge you to stay close to a community who will remind you of the gospel, encourage you to hope, and call you to love. Thank you for joining me on this journey and I look forward to meeting again soon!

Elizabeth
www.livingstorygrace.com

Works Cited

Allender, Dan. *The Wounded Heart: Hope for the Adult Victim of Childhood Sexual Abuse.* Colorado Springs, CO: Navpress, 1987.

Bierma, Nathan L. K. *Bringing Heaven Down to Earth.* Phillipsburg, NJ: P&R Publishing, 2005.

Bridges, Jerry. "Gospel-Driven Sanctification." *Modern Reformation,* May June, 2003.

Buechner, Frederick. *Telling Secrets, A Memoir.* New York, NY: HarperOne, 1991.

Carson, D. A. *Becoming Conversant with the Emerging Church: Understanding a Movement and Its Implications.* Grand Rapids, MI: Zondervan, 2005.

Chapman, Steven Curtis. "Big Story." *All Things New.* Comp. Steven Curtis Chapman. 2004.

Gerkin, C. V. *Widening the Horizons: Pastoral Responses to a Fragmented Society.* Philadelphia, PA: Westminster Press, 1986.

Goheen, Michael. "Reading the Bible as One Story." *Inhabiting the Biblical Story.* Wellington: Victorian University, 2003.

L'Engle, Madeleine. *Walking on Water: Reflections on Faith and Art.* Wheaton, IL: Shaw, 1980.

Lewis, C. S. "'Historicism.'" In *Reflections of C.S. Lewis.* Edited by Walter Hooper. Grand Rapids, MI: Eerdmans, 1995.

Longman, Tremper, and Dan Allender. *Cry of the Soul.* Colorado Springs, CO: Navpress, 1997.

Longman, Tremper. *How to Read the Psalms.* Downer's Grove, IL: Intervarsity Press, 1988.

Packer, J. I. *Concise Theology.* Wheaton, IL: Tyndale, 1993.

Peterson, Eugene. *Conversations: The Message Bible with Its Translator.* Colorado Springs, CO: Navpress, 2007.

—. *Reversed Thunder: The Revelation of John and the Praying Imagination.* New York, NY: HarperCollins, 1988.

Plantinga, Cornelius. *Engaging God's World: A Christian Vision of Faith, Learning, and Living.* Grand Rapids, MI: Eerdmans, 2002.

—. *Not the Way It's Supposed to Be: A Breviary of Sin.* Grand Rapids, MI: Eerdmans, 1995.

Remen, Rachel. *Kitchen-Table Wisdom.* New York, NY: Penguin, 2006.

Smith, Scotty. *The Reign of Grace: The Delights and Demands of God's Love.* West Monroe, LA: Howard Publishing, 2003.

Smith, Scotty, and Steven Curtis Chapman. *Restoring Broken Things.* Nashville, TN: Thomas Nelson, 2007.

Stott, John. *Authentic Christianity: From the Writings of John Stott.* Edited by Timothy Dudley-Smith. Downer's Grove, IL: InterVarsity Press, 1995.

Taylor, Daniel. *The Healing Power of Stories.* New York: Doubleday, 1996.

Tolkien, J. R. R. *The Fellowship of the Ring.* Boston, MA: Houghton Mifflin, 1999.

Tripp, Paul David. *Instruments in the Redeemer's Hands.* Phillipsburg, NJ: P&R Publishing, 2002.

Wolters, Albert, and Michael Goheen. *Creation Regained: Biblical Basics for a Reformational Worldview.* Grand Rapids, MI: Eerdmans, 2005.

Wolterstorff, Nicholas. *Until Justice and Peace Embrace.* Grand Rapids, MI: Eerdmans, 1983.